Haiku Anthology

Insights and Observations

Copyright © 2017
Douglas Paul Creations, LLC

All rights reserved. No part of this book may be reproduced, stored, or transmitted by any means whether auditory, graphic, mechanical, or electronic without written permission of both publisher and author, except in the case of brief excerpts used in critical articles and reviews.
Unauthorized reproduction of any part of this work is illegal and is punishable by law.

ISBN-13: 978-0692849880
ISBN-10: 0692849882

Published by
Douglas Paul Creations, LLC
in cooperation with
FanStory Haiku Club

Table of Contents

Chapter 1: Fire

Chapter 2: Water

Chapter 3: Earth

Chapter 4: Air

Chapter 5: Birds

Chapter 6: Fish

Chapter 7: Amphibians

Chapter 8: Reptiles

Chapter 9: Insects

Chapter 10: Mammals

Chapter 11: Winter

Chapter 12: Spring

Chapter 13: Summer

Chapter 14: Autumn

Chapter 15: Trees

Chapter 16: Flowers

Chapter 17: Vines

Chapter 18: Weeds

Contributing Authors

Douglas Paul
Haiku Society of America
Tanka Society of America

Dean Cook
Haiku Society of America
Tanka Society of America

Robyn Corum
Haiku Society of America

MariVal Bayles
Haiku Society of America

Lura Saluna
Haiku Society of America
Haiku Canada
Tanka Society of America

Michael D. Mann
Haiku Society of America
Tanka Society of America

Kerry Robinson
Haiku Society of America

Christine Watts

Debbie Johnson

Brenda Bickers

Nika

Michael P. Cahill

Karyn Stockwell

Jim Lorson, Sr.

Andre Le Mont Wilson

Teresa Burt

Ray Griffin, Jr.

Trang Diem Nguyen

Ulla McFarlane

Alex Krysyna

lorraine m Benedetto

Giddy Nielsen-Sweep

Barb Henson

Zanya

Jan Lodle

Nome K. Morgan

Forward

HAIKU is a short form of JAPANESE POETRY.
It is typically characterized by three qualities:

1. The juxtaposition of two images or ideas and a cutting word – KIREJI – or punctuation mark between them.

2. Seventeen syllables, in three phrases of 5, 7, and 5 ON, the Japanese voice sound equivalent to our syllables.

3. KIGO, or seasonal reference, usually drawn from a SAIJIKI, which is an extensive list of terms.

Though traditional haiku tend to follow the 17 ON 5/7/5 format and take nature as their subject, modern haiku are increasingly unlikely to follow these tenets, but the use of juxtaposition continues to be honored.

Haiku record an immediate life experience and can be much more than a poetry form. They become an intuitive way of life, of being. Because haiku writing is rooted in experience, the best time to compose a haiku is right after an event. But the experience always comes first! Then, only afterward as it is recalled, as vividly as possible, the experience is put to paper.

Haiku often have a deeper meaning that is not readily apparent on the first reading. They are meant to be read many times to let the meaning unfold into the reader's own personal experience. They are deliberately brief to allow a broad range of interpretation.

I teach haiku classes online at a writers' social site called FanStory. One of my students, Douglas Paul, came up with the brilliant idea of starting a Haiku Club and weekly haiku challenges to promote haiku on FanStory.

Our Haiku Club encourages the art of reading and writing haiku, and provides a place where the FanStory community can come to share their haiku, get ideas, learn new haiku writing skills, and hang out with other haiku poets who enjoy reading and writing haiku.

The club, the weekly challenges, and the creation of this book have provided an environment conducive to the appreciation of haiku and other Japanese poetry. The result has been phenomenal. More people are writing haiku than ever before, and the quality of these haiku has improved dramatically.

This anthology includes 120 of the best haiku written by FanStory Haiku Club poets. Each has been carefully selected to represent this growing community and to share the wonderful gift that is haiku.

We hope you enjoy our anthology. Thank you for reading.

MariVal Bayles
Japanese Poetry Instructor
Member of the Haiku Society of America

Chapter 1
Fire

HAIKU ANTHOLOGY

Nordic warriors
entranced by funeral pyre
spirits soar

~ Dean Cook

virulent coal fire
traps miners beneath the surface –
empty coffins

~ MariVal Bayles

flames lick
maple logs in fireplace
hot syrup

~ Debbie Johnson

lightning erupts
in the midnight sky –
firestorm

~ Douglas Paul

flickering flames
rekindle memories of lost love
ambiance

~ Jan Lodle

Chapter 2
Water

ocean tide pool
captures luminous sea star
I make a wish

~ Karyn Stockwell

INSIGHTS AND OBSERVATIONS

morning tiptoes
along water winding
out to sea

~ Michael D. Mann

bleak and blustery
Old Man Winter huffs and puffs
boreal beauty

~ Dean Cook

a calm eddy
amidst raging rapids —
welcome reprieve

~ Douglas Paul

first morning dew
graces Mount Madonna —
wet ankles

~ MariVal Bayles

Chapter 2
Water

dead sea shipwreck

drowning in sorrow

salty tears

~ Brenda Bickers

INSIGHTS AND OBSERVATIONS

tears of joy
tears of sadness
one river

~ Michael P. Cahill

summer sea
retreats and returns
love's lullaby

~ Nika

predawn hoarfrost
cloaks lawn beneath my feet
grass blades shatter

~ Andre Le Mont Wilson

ominous dark clouds
open with damaging rains —
devastation

~ Jim Lorson, Sr.

Chapter 3
Earth

with relentless love

father plows from dusk 'til dawn –

harvest of the heart

~ MariVal Bayles

the wind brought the scent
of woodlands and piled fresh dirt
perfumes of the earth

~ Michael D. Mann

tree stands alone
too long in barren landscape –
life withdraws

~ Douglas Paul

spoils of war
entombed in sorrow
earth enriched

~ Michael P. Cahill

dry and hot winds blow
relentlessly through the night
barren soil

~ Ulla McFarlane

Chapter 4
Air

industrial plant

adds to global warming

suffocation

~ Lura Saluna

clouds bubble
on horizon into blackened sky
storm brew

~ Teresa Burt

white flakes swirl
as I hike along creek's rocky path
snow globe

~ A. Ray Griffin, Jr.

snow-white jasmine
accents mom's garden –
sweet memories

~ Trang Diem Nguyen

aspen grove
rustles in mountain breeze
summer wind song

~ Karyn Stockwell

Chapter 4
Air

eagle flies fish
towards eaglets' gaping beaks
seafood flown daily

~ Andre Le Mont Wilson

INSIGHTS AND OBSERVATIONS

veil of fog
covers full moon
Luna's eclipsed

~ Debbie Johnson

white petals flutter
to the ground in a light breeze
spring is in the air

~ Ulla McFarlane

warm breeze
caresses mother earth —
breath of life

~ Douglas Paul

wind and sleet
batter bent branches
crows wait for spring

~ Michael D. Mann

Chapter 5
Birds

old owl

observes forest from tree branch –

ancient seer

~ Douglas Paul

eagle soars
over wintry wilderness
silent sojourn

~ Alex Krysyna

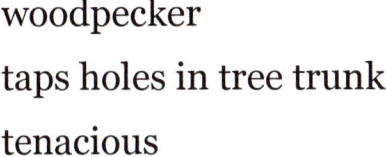

three herons balance
with effortless discipline –
morning yoga class

~ Karyn Stockwell

woodpecker
taps holes in tree trunk
tenacious

~ A. Ray Griffin, Jr.

hawk soars above
silhouettes kite against blue –
no strings attached

~ Christine Watts

Chapter 5
Birds

peacock mating dance
with a fan of love for her –
eyes shimmer

~ Lura Saluna

INSIGHTS AND OBSERVATIONS

crows coldly conspire
to display strength in numbers –
murder most fowl

~ Dean Cook

minnow struggles
in kingfisher's beak –
ice fishing

~ Michael D. Mann

plump round robin
posing on cherry tree limb
nuptials commence

~ lorraine m Benedetto

plate glass window
looks like clear skies –
flat bird

~ Robyn Corum

Chapter 6
Fish

below plum blossoms

koi swims gracefully at dusk–

today surrenders

~ MariVal Bayles

INSIGHTS AND OBSERVATIONS

silver salmon
return upstream to spawn –
grizzly death awaits

~ Douglas Paul

side by side
father baits son's hook
catching memories

~ Robyn Corum

stringer of trout
on a rainy afternoon –
fisherman's rainbow

~ Debbie Johnson

seen through cold drizzle
goldfish glint and glitter –
sunken treasures

~ Andre Le Mont Wilson

Chapter 7
Amphibians

tree frog lies low

beneath umbrella leaves –

sheltered life

~ MariVal Bayles

INSIGHTS AND OBSERVATIONS

alligator newt
land and pond dweller –
poisonous nip

~ Lura Saluna

adorable
mudpuppies and waterdogs –
vicious carnivores

~ Robyn Corum

tree frog's eggs hatch
on forest leaf over pond
tadpole's waterslide

~ Karyn Stockwell

wind whirls over wet rocks
frogs sing

~ Michael D. Mann

Chapter 8
Reptiles

thorny devil lizard

eats ants Down Under –

tiny tank

~ Lura Saluna

INSIGHTS AND OBSERVATIONS

serpent slithers
upon Eden's green fields –
sinful pleasures

~ MariVal Bayles

newborn turtles
scamper from sand to sea
instinctive journey

~ Karyn Stockwell

boa constrictor
coils around chosen prey –
deadly hug

~ Douglas Paul

sexy snakes slither
over grass and through glades
legless sensation

~ Nome K. Morgan

Chapter 9
Insects

lights flicker

as fireflies frolic –

tiny galaxy

~ Douglas Paul

INSIGHTS AND OBSERVATIONS

time turns hope to dust
— termites do the same

~ Robyn Corum

ladybug eats
aphids from flower stems —
nature's pesticide

~ Lura Saluna

grapevine moth
partakes in daily tours
free wine taste

~ Christine Watts

winter days,
lone ladybug comes inside —
welcomed seasonal guest

~ Trang Diem Nguyen

Chapter 9
Insects

orchid mantis...

looks like a flower

waits for prey

~ Michael D. Mann

INSIGHTS AND OBSERVATIONS

wicked wasp
decorates domicile with dead
fetid Feng Shui

~ Dean Cook

busy bees flitter
among flowers with a buzz
nectar of life

~ Ulla McFarlane

praying mantis
mates then devours her partner
sex and dinner

~ Karyn Stockwell

where lilies blossom.
locusts gather at
shallow stream –
rest stop

~ MarVal Bayles

Chapter 10
Mammals

majestic panther
stalks prey in the dark –
stealth night moves

~ MariVal Bayles

INSIGHTS AND OBSERVATIONS

bamboo grows green
for thirteen moon cycles –
panda treats

~ Lura Saluna

wild wolf
howls at the full moon –
lunar lament

~ Douglas Paul

with sharp painted claws
she stalks concrete jungle:
cougar

~ Robyn Corum

red kangaroos
box their way to final round
winner takes the doe

~ Christine Watts

Chapter 11
Winter

old woman shivers,

bent by her load –

weight of wisdom

~ Robyn Corum

INSIGHTS AND OBSERVATIONS

hearth fire glows
during a winter evening —
a lonely cat naps

~ Trang Diem Nguyen

ice fishers
reel in yellow walleye
fresh frozen

~ A. Ray Griffin, Jr.

I've lost direction
in this endless snowfield
my tangled mind

~ Giddy Nielsen-Sweep

winter blizzard
isolates mountain cabin
wish we were there

~ Karyn Stockwell

Chapter 11
Winter

freezing rain falls
coats tree limbs with ice—
fatal beauty

~ Douglas Paul

INSIGHTS AND OBSERVATIONS

blizzard blusters in
with frightful frigid fury
inhospitable

~ Dean Cook

homeless and asleep
on a white bed of winter –
dead of night

~ Lura Saluna

dead and dried evergreen
lies on the snow-covered road –
echoes of laughter

~ MariVal Bayles

branches of bare trees
etch spectres on dark skyline
wintry tapestry

~ Zanya

Chapter 12
Spring

spring surprises

with waft of sweet lilac –

magical

~ Trang Diem Nguyen

INSIGHTS AND OBSERVATIONS

fledglings fight for food
only the strong survive –
avian love

~ Michael D. Mann

bear awakens
from deep slumber –
call of spring

~ Douglas Paul

grape hyacinths
encapsulated by late snow –
chilled wine

~ Teresa Burt

robins gather
for early morning breakfast
lawn party

~ Karyn Stockwell

Chapter 12
Spring

gentle spring breezes
brush bare branches –
zenful pleasures

~ Dean Cook

INSIGHTS AND OBSERVATIONS

baby robin eggs
a Mother's Day surprise
Spring!

~ Kerry Robinson

hazy moon reflects
no light, yet I still see –
love in your eyes

~ Giddy Nielsen-Sweep

yellow daffodils
spring to life in my garden –
ah-choo!

~ Lura Saluna

spring cleaning on hold
the vacuum is broken –
that sucks

~ Barb Henson

Chapter 13
Summer

kids cannonball
off rope at lake's edge –
school's out

~ Karyn Stockwell

INSIGHTS AND OBSERVATIONS

soft breeze
on my tulips –
whispers

~ Kerry Robinson

sweet summertime dreams
melt miles until I'm with you –
anticipation

~ Dean Cook

relentless sunlight
filters through tree branches –
shadows dance

~ Douglas Paul

inebriated
on sweet honeysuckle scent –
summer snookered

~ MariVal Bayles

Chapter 13
Summer

orange tree blossoms,

a treat for all to enjoy –

juicy decadence

~ Lura Saluna

INSIGHTS AND OBSERVATIONS

far from floral fields
a bee dies on my porch
farewell sweet summer

~ Andre Le Mont Wilson

it's gone
when I see it
sand crab

~ Robyn Corum

sultry days
must find relief
from myself

~ Giddy Nielsen-Sweep

shortest night into
the longest day of summer
sunbather's heaven

~ Michael D. Mann

Chapter 14
Autumn

crickets chirp softly
in barren fields, rife with frost –
Autumn descends

~ Dean Cook

INSIGHTS AND OBSERVATIONS

whirling currents
in chilly wind gusts
summer's send off

~ Giddy Neilsen-Sweep

empty swing
sways in Autumn breeze
school begins

~ Karyn Stockwell

backyard bonfires
beneath skeletal trees:
s'more, please

~ Robyn Corum

chestnuts ripe
with flavor from the tree –
turkey's delight

~ Lura Saluna

Chapter 14
Autumn

Autumn...

technicolor nature

one leaf at a time

~ Michael D. Mann

golden leaves
adorn the mighty oak trees –
crown of Autumn

~ Douglas Paul

colored rain of leaves
floating through air –
lays golden blankets

~ Kerry Robinson

loyal hound runs
ahead to flush the fox –
crisp Autumn morn

~ MariVal Bayles

feathered friends fly
south to warmer climate –
frost warning

~ Teresa Burt

Chapter 15
Trees

rainbow eucalyptus

appeals to the senses –

nature's masterpiece

~ MariVal Bayles

frosty winds whine
whilst sparse branches whisper –
echoes of a soul

~ Dean Cook

morning birds gather
on flowering magnolia
hallelujah choir

~ Karyn Stockwell

diffused light
shines softly through green canopy
majestic new life

~ Ulla McFarlane

mighty oak
bows his head –
as wind passes by

~ Kerry Robinson

Chapter 15
Trees

who knows

what rapport they share –

trees and birds

~ Giddy Nielsen-Sweep

INSIGHTS AND OBSERVATIONS

soul weeps
under willow's comfort
tender tears

~ Alex Krysyna

tall red woods
reach for the sky –
majestic forest

~ Douglas Paul

bamboo limb
quivers from the weight
of a bird

~ Michael D. Mann

trees tall and stoic
live for centuries –
keepers of the past

~ Lura Saluna

Chapter 16
Flowers

perched on sticks
birds of paradise –
bask in sun

~ Kerry Robinson

rose petals fall
as blush of spring fades –
love grows cold

~ Douglas Paul

overflowing with
spring blessings –
buttercups

~ Robyn Corum

marbled nude's
head bows towards lavender pansies
graciousness

~ A. Ray Griffin, Jr.

wind and snow
has even withered
the pampas grass

~ Giddy Nielsen-Sweep

Chapter 16
Flowers

all aflutter...

hummingbirds and Monarchs –

kissing flowers

~ Michael D. Mann

INSIGHTS AND OBSERVATIONS

perfect rose
blooms in admired splendor
effortless life

~ Michael P. Cahill

child holds buttercup
under chin for gold luster
butter lover

~ Karyn Stockwell

Corpse flowers bloom
to mimic death's pungency —
botanists make a big stink

~Dean Cook

sweet love's compassion
the Lotus Flower
honey bee's delight

~ Lura Saluna

Chapter 17
Vines

rainforest

jungle vines –

monkey's playground

~ Kerry Robinson

INSIGHTS AND OBSERVATIONS

Morning Glories
awaken at early dawn –
nightly sleeper

~ Nome K. Morgan

melancholic thoughts
looking at intertwined vines –
tangled up in blue

~ MariVal Bayles

trumpet vines spread
changing all colors to green-
redecorating

~ Barb Henson

endless sweat
coaxes sweetness to the vine
chugalug

~ Michael P. Cahill

Chapter 17
Vines

overgrowth of vines

consumes crumbling brick wall

tangled in time

~ Teresa Burt

hummingbirds gather
at trumpet vine's flowered cups
nectar bar

~ Karyn Stockwell

a single tendril
guides large vine to higher height –
effective leader

~ Trang Diem Nguyen

hours from ivy
lawn snail camps two feet away
weary traveler

~ Andre Le Mont Wilson

cluster of grapes
matures on the vine –
wine glass awaits

~ Douglas Paul

Chapter 18
Weeds

red blight
in weed garden
haughty rose

~ Michael P. Cahill

INSIGHTS AND OBSERVATIONS

milkweed attracts
monarch butterflies –
ditch art

~ Lura Saluna

weeds grow
immune to drought and heat –
relentless life force

~ Douglas Paul

dad's bindweed
is son's morning glory –
new perspective

~ MariVal Bayles

dandelions
picked with love by toddler
mommy's first bouquet

~ Karyn Stockwell

Chapter 18
Weeds

dandelion crown

on my young head

wistful memories

~ Nome K. Morgan

INSIGHTS AND OBSERVATIONS

dandelion wine...
from weed to exotic drink
family secret

~ Michael D. Mann

always there
in the garden pulling weeds
she sheds her anger

~ Giddy Nielsen-Sweep

buried Down Under
Hairy Panic weed takes hold –
apocalyptic

~ Dean Cook

kudzu devours acres
of hardwood –
living lava

~ Robyn Corum

Acknowledgements

The FanStory Community
Haiku Club

Members of the Board:
Douglas Paul
MariVal Bayles
Robyn Corum
Lura Saluna
Dean Cook
Michael D. Mann
Michael P. Cahill

Contributing Members
Alex Krysyna
Christine Watts